MONEY MATTERS

HOW TO BECOME A SMART CONSUMER

Written by Katherine Howe and Judith Edelstein
Illustrated by Mary Lou Johnson

GRADES 4–6

Edited by Dianne Draze and Sonsie Conroy
Published by Prufrock Press Inc.

Printed in the United States of America.

ISBN-13 978-1-59363-108-6
ISBN-10 1-59363-108-1

Prufrock Press, Inc.
P.O. Box 8813
Waco, Texas 76714-8813
(800) 998-2208
Fax (800) 240-0333
http://www.prufrock.com

Contents

Information for the Instructor

Money and credit are important elements of our everyday lives. Even young children are aware of the fact that money has value; that is, it can be used to purchase things we want, it can impress other people, and, if not managed well, it can create financial problems.

Researchers who track spending patterns report that children and teenagers spend hundreds of billions of dollars a year and influence billions of dollars of household purchases for their families. While the impact of these financial decisions is considerable, looking toward a time when they will be adults, they will be making even larger economic decisions that will affect their well being as well as that of their families. It is pertinent, therefore, that youngsters begin learning how to be smart consumers and how to make good economic decisions. Once they are aware of factors that influence their buying decisions, they will be better consumers and have the skills to avoid possible financial problems as adults.

"A fool and his money are soon parted" (old English proverb). The good news is that we don't have to be fools about our money. People can be trained to recognize forces that affect their spending and to make wise economic decisions. This unit is the beginning of a life-long learning process. Its focus is building awareness of each student's impact as a consumer. In the process of completing the activities, students will gain an understanding of the effects of consumer decisions on their own lives, their families, the community and society. With this basic information, they will be able to approach all future purchasing decisions with the ability to ask the right questions, to analyze their own motivations, and to recognize what options are available to them.

As a result of completing the activities in this unit, students will:

- become familiar with the history of money and the different monetary instruments
- become familiar with the terminology used by consumers
- analyze personal spending habits
- identify advertising techniques that affect purchasing decisions
- make a personal budget
- be able to determine the cost of buying on credit
- investigate the various factors that motivate consumer purchases
- investigate how supply and demand establish prices
- differentiate between luxuries and necessities
- understand the three major economic systems
- analyze the interdependence between consumer and producer in our economic system
- write checks and balance a check ledger
- gather information about products and services to determine the best buy before shopping

This book provides an easy-to-use format that incorporates several different ways to present information. **Lesson plans** provide step-by-step instructions for group lessons. Each lesson also has a list of suggested **extensions** for projects that will give students opportunities to present their knowledge in creative ways. **Worksheets** are reproducible pages that present information about different aspects of consumerism and either provide ways to apply knowledge or guidelines for projects. As a whole, this unit is a complete guide for introducing students to all the most important concepts in consumerism.

Group Lessons

Lesson 1 - What is Money?

Objective

Students will identify the characteristics of things that have been used for money.

Materials
Worksheet entitled "What is Money?, page 17.

Procedure
1. Introduce this unit by discussing the concept of money and how it evolved. In addition to the information provided on the suggested worksheet, you may want to add the following:

   - Barter is a difficult economic system because it is dependent on a person wanting what the other person is offering and on the items offered for trade being of equal value.
   - To get what was needed, people often had to make three-party (or more) trades in a barter system.
   - In a money economy goods and services are exchanged through the use of money that has a standardized monetary value.
   - Almost anything that is valued can be used as money. Cattle constituted the earliest form of money.
   - Eventually precious metals like gold and silver replaced direct bartering of goods and services.
   - In the modern world gold and silver have been replaced by paper fiduciary money (checks, bank notes, government issues), credit cards, and electronic transfers.
   - In ancient times the temples served as banks and priests were the bankers. They provided safekeeping of people's money and also lent money.
   - Money was first coined in Greece in about 700 B.C. Paper bills were introduced in China in the ninth century but were not used in Europe until the seventeenth century.
   - The Romans adopted the Greeks' banking system, made it more uniform and spread it to other countries that they conquered.
   - From the thirteenth to the sixteenth centuries, the majority of banking firms were Italian.

2. Choose something that you could use as a classroom currency. Discuss:
   - How you would value different items?
   - What are some possible problems with this currency?
   - What would happen if you wanted to buy something from another classroom and they used something different for their currency?

3. Discuss what problems would exist if all money was in the form of gold.

4. Discuss the problems that might exist if each state (province, city) had its own currency.

Lesson 2 - Spending Choices

Objective
Students will analyze their own spending habits.

Materials
Worksheets entitled, "Ten Things I Love To Do," "You Can't Have It All," "Money Decisions," and "My Financial Personality," pages 19, 20, 21, and 22.

Procedure
1. Pass out the worksheet entitled "Ten Things I Love to Do," page 19. Have students quickly write the ten things that they most like to do. After they have made their lists, have them make a mark by those things that cost money and write an estimated cost. Then have students add up the costs of their activities. Discuss what activities students have listed and what differences exist in their totals. Follow up by having students evaluate their spending habits by writing what they learned about themselves from this exercise what changes they might like to make in their spending habits.

2. Pass out the worksheet "You Can't Have It All" and discuss the idea of choice — how consumers have to make choices about how

they will spend their money, and producers have to make decisions about what they will produce. There are very few people who have so much money that they do not have to make some tradeoffs.

3. Using the "Money Decisions" worksheet, have students indicate what purchasing decisions they would make in various situations.

4. Using the "My Financial Personality" worksheet, have students assess their earning and spending habits.

Extensions

Descriptive Words - Give each student a piece of construction paper that is in the shape of a coin or a dollar sign. On the cutout, have each person write words that describe how he or she sees himself or herself as a consumer.

List - Ask students to discuss spending habits with their friends, parents, and neighbors. After gathering first-hand information, they should make a list of at least ten common harmful spending habits.

Lesson 3 - Wants and Needs

Objective
Students will be able to distinguish between a luxury and a necessity.

Materials
Worksheets entitled "Wants and Needs," and "You're a Millionaire," pages 23 and 24.

Procedure
1. As a class, discuss the difference between necessities (those things you need) and luxuries (those things you want but don't actually need). Make a list of necessities and a list of luxuries.

2. Complete worksheet, "Wants and Needs," page 23.

Extensions

Collage - Divide the class into small groups. Have each group cut out pictures from magazines and mount the pictures in a collage that shows the two classifications of spending, ne-

cessities and luxuries. Have each group show their collage and explain their classifications.

Family Expenditures - Ask students to talk to their parents about their family budgets and identify which expenditures are for necessities and which are for luxuries.

A Million Dollars - Have students complete the worksheet "You're a Millionaire," page 24.

Lesson 4 - Budgets

Objective
Students will make a budget that reflects a month of income and expenses.

Materials

Worksheets entitled "Your Budget," and "A Family Budget," pages 25 and 26.

Procedure
1. Discuss the fact that budgets are spending plans that project income and expenditures. They are used by individuals, families, businesses, and governments. A budget is one tool a good money manager uses.

2. As a class, make a list of the major categories on which students spend their money. These categories might include food, entertainment, clothes, sports equipment, games, books, and savings.

3. Discuss the advantages of having a budget. This might include being able to save for bigger purchases or occasional expenses, not running out of money before the end of the month, being able to account for money and know in which categories you spend money, being able to set aside some money for savings, or keeping impulse purchasing in line.

4. On the budget sheet, have students write down how much money they have to spend each month and also estimate how much money they usually spend in each category during a typical month.

5. Then have each student keep track of the money they spend for a month. They should keep a log of everything they spend and at the end of the month, they should total their expenditures and compare their actual expenditures to the budgeted figures.

Extensions

Family Budget - Either individually or in small groups use the worksheet entitled "A Family Budget" (page 26) to create a monthly budget for a family of four. You will give students an income with which to work. The budget should realistically reflect the cost of housing, utilities, transportation, food and health care for your community.

Record Keeping Forms - Have students design sets of forms that will enable their families to keep track of their monthly incomes and expenditures.

Saving Money - In small groups, have students brainstorm ideas for saving money.

Lesson 5 - Packaging Analysis

Objective
Students will be able to analyze product packaging and its impact on purchasing decisions.

Materials
products brought from home, cereal boxes, "Packaging Analysis," "You Pay for Convenience," and "Reading the Labels" worksheets, pages 27, 28, 29 and 30.

Procedure
1. Ask students to bring in a product from home. The product should be in its original package.

2. As a group, analyze the packaging of the products. Discuss the following things:

   - How does the design of the package or the words on the package convince someone to buy it?
   - What colors are used most often in packaging?
   - What do the words "new," "improved," or "extra cleaning power" mean to the consumer?
   - What would be the effect of using the opposite words — "old," "just enough cleaning power?"
   - Is packaging different if it is intended to appeal to children rather than adults?

3. Make a list of things that make packages attractive to consumers.

4. (optional) Take two or three varieties of the same product (like three brands of beans). Discuss the following questions:

   - What does each of the packages tell you about the product?
   - What feelings do the packages project?
   - Which product looks like the best quality?
   - Which one would you buy? Why?

5. Divide the class into groups and have them work together to analyze cereal packages using the worksheet "Packaging Analysis" as a guide.

Extensions
Package Design - Ask students to cover a can or a box with white paper. Then have them design their own package for a product. Save the package for use with lesson 7.

Convenience Foods - Have students compare the cost of convenience foods by completing the worksheet "You Pay for Convenience," page 29.

Reading Labels - Encourage students to read the labels to obtain nutritional information and product pricing by completing the worksheet "Reading the Labels," page 30.

Lesson 6 - Advertising Techniques

Objective
Students will identify factors that affect consumers' decisions to purchase various products.

Materials
magazines

Procedure
1. Review the concept of luxuries and necessities. List some luxuries and some necessities.

2. Discuss the following:

   - What do manufacturers and advertising agencies do to convince people to buy their products?
   - Do companies selling necessities use the same tactics as companies selling luxuries?

- How do companies selling luxuries convince you to buy things that you really don't need?

3. Present the following advertising techniques. Ask students to supply examples of each type of advertising.
   - bandwagon - everyone is doing it
   - testimonial - endorsement by a famous person or authority
   - image - the product is associated with certain people, places, sounds, or activities
   - appeal to human needs - claims that use of the product will supply health and well-being, security, approval, beauty, comfort, or pleasure

4. Discuss which of these techniques is most convincing to students.

5. Divide students into groups of two to four people. Pass out magazines and ask each group to find three advertisements and identify the advertising techniques used.

Extension

Advertisements - Have students create advertisements for items that are popular with their age group using one of the advertising techniques you discussed during the lesson.

Lesson 7 - Creating Advertisements

Objective
Students will apply their knowledge of advertising techniques by writing convincing advertising copy.

Materials
paper, pens, packages from Lesson 5

Procedure
1. Have students write a list of descriptive words for the packages they created in lesson 5.

2. Then have them describe the appeal this product would have for consumers by answering the question, "Why would anyone want to buy this product?"

3. Have them use these ideas and descriptive words to write advertising copy that would be used in a printed advertisement or description for this product.

4. After copy has been edited and revised, have them neatly copy the text and display the advertising copy with the product packages.

Lesson 8 - Mass Media

Objective
Students will identify different ways to advertise a product and determine which ways are most effective for specific purposes.

Materials
paper, pencil

Procedure
1. Ask, "Where do we see advertising?" Make a list of all the ideas suggested.

2. Define mass media as a means of communication that reaches a large number of people (newspapers, radio, television, magazines, etc.). Choose a product and brainstorm how this product could be sold without using the mass media.

3. Discuss the following, taking into consideration mass media and all other forms of advertising your class has discussed:
   - Which of these ways of advertising products would be the most effective for the product you have chosen for your brainstorming session?
   - Which would work best for reaching school-age children? parents? elderly people?
   - Which would work best for selling food? clothes? services? computers? books? athletic equipment?

4. Have students write a paragraph explaining how they are personally affected by advertising; that is, how advertising influences their purchasing decisions. In the paragraph, they should explain which form of advertising influences them the most.

Lesson 9 - Supply and Demand

Objective
Students will determine the effects of supply and demand on prices.

Materials
"Supply and Demand" and "To Market, To Market" worksheets, pages 31 and 32.

Procedure
1. Use the following questions to guide a discussion about supply and demand:

   - Which costs more, gold or sand? Why?
   - What if sand were scarce?
   - What other things (besides sand) would cost more?
   - What if we found a cheap, plentiful replacement for sand?
   - If the most popular toy this year costs $20.00, what would happen to the price if everyone wanted one but the toy store could only get a limited supply?
   - If the toy store orders a large order of this toy but in the meantime another toy manufacturer comes out with a new and better version of the toy that all the children will want, what happens to the price of the first toy?

2. Discuss how supply and demand determines pricing. Scarcity and demand will both drive the price of an item higher, while a surplus or lack of demand will cause the price to lower.

3. Discuss examples from real life when demand (or scarcity) has driven up the price of items or when an oversupply has driven down the price.

4. Have students complete the worksheet entitled "Supply and Demand," page 31.

Answers - Law of Supply - Arrows for price and supply point the same direction. Price and the quantity supplied are directly related.
Law of Demand - Arrows for price and demand point in the opposite direction. The price and quantity demanded are inversely related.

Extension

Production Analysis - Discuss how many people are responsible for bringing an item to market. Using the worksheet "To Market, To Market" have students trace the steps it takes to get a product to market.

Lesson 10 - Credit and Interest

Objective
Students will demonstrate their understanding of credit and interest by calculating credit charges on various purchases and determining the best way to buy the items.

Materials
"Buying on Credit" worksheet, page 33.

Procedure
1. Ask, "What do you do if you need to buy something and you don't have enough money?"

2. Continue the discussion, incorporating the following concepts:

   - Credit is the purchase of goods and services by delayed payment.
   - Consumer credit is a loan that is made to a consumer to facilitate a purchase. This is usually made by the store that is making the sale. It may also include credit that is extended to consumers through the use of credit cards.
   - Bank credit is a loan that is made by the bank to one of its customers. This may be for large or small purchases.
   - Credit is usually used for large purchases that would be difficult to handle with cash, like homes and cars.
   - Collateral is some tangible property that the borrower offers the lender as security for the loan. If the loan is not repaid on the agreed schedule, the institution making the loan has a right to take possession of the collateral. In the case of a mortgage, the land or building is usually the collateral. In an automobile loan, the car is the collateral.
   - Unsecured loans do not involve collateral. These are usually for smaller purchases.
   - The cost of credit (interest) varies. It can be very expensive, depending on the lender and its terms.

3. Discuss situations when it is necessary or advantageous to borrow money and when spending money you don't have causes problems.

4. Introduce the concept of interest, a fee for the use of the money. Discuss the fact that different interest rates are charged by banks,

lending institutions, credit card companies, check cashing companies and stores.

5. Show students how to figure the amount of interest that must be paid on the money borrowed. Show them that you multiply the **rate** times the **principle** (amount borrowed) times the **time** for which the money is being borrowed (I = P x R x T). Time is figured in fractions of a year. Interest on $1000 loan at 5% for 6 months would be
I = 1000 x .05 x 6/12 = $25.
This means that the person borrowing the money would end up paying back the amount of the loan ($1000) plus the amount of interest for half a year ($25) for a total of $1025.

6. Give students some of the following problems.

   - $300 loan at 6% interest for 1 year
     (300 x .06 x 1 = 18)
   - $800 loan at 10% interest for 2 years
     (800 x .10 x 2 = 160)
   - $500 loan at 12% interest for 6 months
     (500 x .12 x 6/12 = 30)
   - $2000 loan at 18% interest for 2 months
     (2000 x .18 x 2/12 = 60)
   - $1500 loan at 9% interest for 2 years 6 months
     (1500 x .09 x 30/12 = 337.50) or
     (1500 x .09 x 2.5 = 337.50)

7. Have students do the worksheet entitled "Buying on Credit," page 33.

Extensions

Chart - Have students investigate what interest rates are charged by various lending institutions (banks, savings and loans, credit cards, and check cashing services). Then have them make a chart that shows the average interest charged by each type of lender.

Paragraph - Have students write a paragraph that explains what types of purchases people usually buy on credit, when it is good to use credit, and some things that are bad about buying on credit.

Lesson 11 - Check Writing

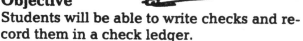

Objective
Students will be able to write checks and record them in a check ledger.

Materials
transparency of sample check, page 34, "Let's Check It Out" worksheets, pages 35-38.

Procedure
1. Discuss checking accounts as a way to keep money safe in the bank and still have access to it. Explain that banks usually charge for using checking accounts. These charges can be a per check charge and/or a monthly charge. People use checking accounts, though, because they are convenient, they are an efficient, safe way of paying bills when the payment must be sent to a distant office, and they are a way of keeping track of expenditures for budgeting and/or taxes.

2. Make a transparency of the sample check on page 34. Go through the different information that is required on a check and how it is recorded.

3. Have students practice writing checks and recording them on a ledger by doing the worksheets entitled "Let's Check It Out," pages 35-38.

Answers
The ledger should have the following balances:

beginning balance	**750.00**
check 101	-323.00
balance	**427.00**
check 102	-236.75
balance	**190.25**
deposit	410.39
balance	**600.64**
check 103	-496.50
balance	**104.14**
deposit	500.00
balance	**604.14**
check 104	-329.62
balance	**274.52**
check 105	-52.52
balance	**222.00**

Lesson 12 - Smart Buying

Objective
Students will apply knowledge of consumer practices by completing one of five projects.

Materials
Worksheet entitled "Smart Buying", page 39 and 40, newspapers, catalogs, "Complaints," "Ordering by Mail," "Shopping on the Internet," and "Rent or Buy?" worksheets, pages 41, 42, 43 and 44.

Procedure
1. Ask students to choose one of the five projects listed below. They should research the market for the best buy and present their findings to the class. The projects are outlined in detail on pages 39 and 40. For each project, you will provide the amount of money they have to spend on the project.

Closet Clean Out
Students will be given money to buy a new wardrobe. They should establish what articles of clothing they need and then find where they can find the best quality for the best price.

Car
You will give students an amount they may spend on their car purchase. Within this budget, they may buy a new or used car. They should establish what their needs are (size, style, upkeep expense) and should consult consumer reports or car magazines for information that will help them make their decisions. They should present their criteria for buying a car as well as the model they finally decide to buy and where they will purchase the car.

Bedroom Design
You will give students an amount they may spend on redecorating their bedrooms. They may not structurally alter the shape or size of their present room, but they may paint, wallpaper, change furniture and furnishings. They should present a floor plan of their remodeled room. This plan should show the changes they would like to make as well as a cost analysis of all the materials and furnishings they will buy.

Vacation Time
You will give students a specific amount of money to use for a week-long vacation for four people. They are to choose a place to visit and figure all expenses for travel, lodging, meals, entrance fees, and any special equipment they may need to buy or rent. Some of the information for prices of lodging can be found on the Internet. In their final presentation, they will describe their destination and itemize all expenses.

Electronic Equipment
You will give students an amount of money they can spend on a sound system. They should visit several retailers in your area or check advertisements in newspapers, catalogs, or the Internet. Based on this information, they should decide which system to buy.

2. When projects are completed, the class should discuss using cash or credit for making their purchases. They should use the formula for calculating simple interest ($I = P \times R \times T$) to find the actual price of their purchases if they were to buy them on credit. As a group, list the advantages and disadvantages of purchasing on credit.

Extensions

Complaints - Students need to know what to do if their purchases do not measure up to expectations. Using the worksheet entitled "Complaints," page 41, review the procedures for lodging product complaints. Then have students do one of the projects.

Other Shopping Sources - Introduce students to things they need to know about shopping by mail or via the Internet by using the pages entitled "Ordering by Mail" and "Shopping on the Internet," pages 42 and 43.

Renting - Using the worksheet entitled "Rent or Buy," page 44, introduce students to the option of renting merchandise rather than buying it.

Lesson 13 - Economic Systems (optional)

Objective
Students will be able to distinguish between the three different economic systems.

Materials
"Economic Systems" worksheet, page 45.

Procedure
1. Ask students, "What would happen if the government owned all stores, farms, manufacturing, and housing, everyone worked for the government, bought things they needed from the government at fixed prices, collected their paychecks from the government and was provided housing and health care by the government?"
   On the other hand, "What would happen if the government didn't interfere in economic life at all? That is, there were no minimum wages, no social security, no standards for safety and sanitation. People could make anything they wanted, wherever they wanted, charge any price they thought people would pay, and treat their employees any way they wanted?"

2. Present information about the three major economic systems — capitalism, communism, and socialism. Discuss the three economic systems. Present the following information:

   - **Capitalism** is an economic system based on private ownership and free enterprise. This system provides for private ownership of resources and production facilities and assumes that as these owners strive to make the largest possible profits that they will produce what consumers want and will use resources efficiently. The government plays a very small role in the economy. All means of production and distribution, like raw materials, land, factories, railroads, airlines, and stores, are privately owned and operated for profit. Typically this system has tended to produce a small group of wealthy people who control most economic activity.
   - **Socialism** is an economic system in which the major share of large-scale resources for production are owned by the state or agencies of the government. This system claims that greater production is possible when individual ownership is replaced by the more-efficient public ownership and that it results in a more equitable division of goods and services. This system results in a much more equal standard of living for all people than the capitalistic system.
   - **Communism** is an economic system in which the ownership of all property is by the whole community. This means that all production and distribution of goods and services are controlled by the community (i.e. government) and all members of the community share in the work and the profits or products that are produced. All housing is held collectively. Communism shares some of the principles of socialism and it is sometimes difficult to find a hard dividing line between the two systems.
   - There are few, if any, totally capitalistic or communistic economies. Most capitalistic economies have some government intervention and ownership. Even in communistic economies people trade, barter, and sell merchandise on a small scale.

3. Discuss the three economic systems, pointing out how each system would handle:

   - ownership of resources
   - manufacturing
   - ownership of distribution means (transportation, railroads, stores, etc.)
   - wages of workers
   - health care, welfare, education
   - distribution of profits from businesses
   - ownership of housing and business facilities
   - decisions about which products to produce and how much to produce
   - decisions about pricing of products
   - how citizens spend their money

4. Discuss the fact that most countries have an economic system that is not strictly one system or another but is a blend of two systems. Identify the features of our country's economic system.

5. Have students do the worksheet entitled "Economic Systems", page 45.

Money Matters Vocabulary

Write a definition for each of these terms.

advertising _____

_____

barter _____

_____

budget _____

_____

collateral _____

_____

comparison shopping _____

_____

consumer _____

_____

credit _____

_____

debt _____

_____

discount _____

_____

guarantee _____

_____

interest _____

_____

Vocabulary, continued

list price ____

____

loan ____

____

luxury ____

____

marketing ____

____

mass media ____

____

necessity ____

____

profit ____

____

retail ____

____

sale ____

____

supply and demand ____

____

wholesale ____

____

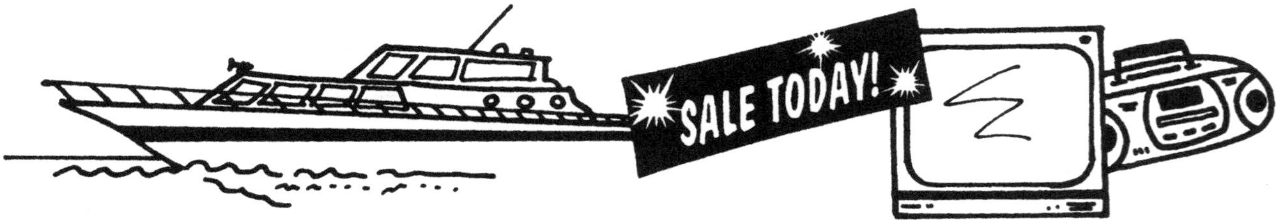

What is Money?

Before there was money, people got what they needed through barter. Barter is the direct exchange of goods or services for other goods and services. This system does not involve money. It is dependent on someone being willing to swap something they have for something that someone else is offering. If they do not want what is being offered, they may have to go through a number of intermediate exchanges to get what they do want. Barter is not as efficient an economic system as using a common medium of exchange, and because it was hard to establish value for all the different items that were traded, people eventually agreed that certain items would be accepted as a medium of exchange and an indiction of value.

In the strictest definition, money is metal pieces that are stamped by the government that has the authority to issue the coins and establish their value. In a more general sense, money is anything a society thinks has value. It is anything that is used as a medium of exchange, a measure of wealth, or a means of payment. Many different things have been used as money, including trading beads, cowrie shell belts, nuts, knives, copper, blocks of salt, large stones, precious stones, fish hooks, nails, tea, and livestock. Most of these forms of money were things that were available in the environment where people lived and that were considered important. Gradually metal (especially gold) was accepted because it was durable, easy to handle, and could be divided into smaller pieces.

For something to be a good medium of exchange, it needs to have most of the following characteristics.
- People must have confidence in it and be able to agree on its value.
- It must be relatively scarce.
- It must be durable.
- It must be easy to store.
- It should be relatively portable.
- It must be hard to reproduce or duplicate.
- It should be able to be divided into smaller pieces.

For the sake of convenience, we accept other forms of payment that represent precious metals. These forms of money are paper money, checks, and credit cards. People accept them as having the same value as metal coins even though the paper in a dollar bill or a check has very little value itself.

$pecial Projects

1. Choose five of the things that people have used for money. For each one, indicate which of the following attributes the particular form of money had.
   - confidence
   - scarcity
   - durable
   - divisible
   - easy to store
   - portable
   - hard to duplicate

   Based on this analysis, which forms of money are the best?

2. Make a cartoon that shows how barter works. List the advantages and disadvantages of barter.

3. Make a list of articles, special talents, and services that you would be willing to exchange for something you wanted. Make an advertisement to publicize what you have to offer.

4. Organize a swap or barter day for your classroom. When you are finished, evaluate the results. What are the advantages and disadvantages of swapping? What might be some ways that people could make contact with other people wanting to swap?

5. Do additional research and then make a poster or display of different things people have used for money.

Ten Things I Love To Do

As quickly as you can, list ten things that you love to do. After you have completed your list, check each activity that involves spending money. Then write how much that activity costs. Finally, add up all the costs to find a total cost for the things you most like to do.

Things I love to do	☑ costs money?	cost
1. _____	☐	_____
2. _____	☐	_____
3. _____	☐	_____
4. _____	☐	_____
5. _____	☐	_____
6. _____	☐	_____
7. _____	☐	_____
8. _____	☐	_____
9. _____	☐	_____
10. _____	☐	_____
	Total cost	_____

What does this show about you and the things you like to do? _____

_____

_____

What, if any, changes do you think you could make if you wanted to save money?_____

_____

_____

You Can't Have It All

Choice and scarcity are fundamental ideas in economics. There are choices that both the consumer and the producer must make. These choices are the result of having limited resources and limited money.

Producers try to make products that will produce the greatest profits. Because land, raw materials, labor, skills, and money are all limited, manufacturers must make choices about:

- what will be produced
- how much will be produced
- where it will be produced
- what price will be charged

Consumers, on the other hand, also have choices to make. Consumers usually adjust their spending to make the most of the money they have available. Since they generally have a limited amount of money to spend on goods, they must decide between spending their money on:

- different goods
- material things or leisure activities
- things for present consumption or for future consumption
- things for themselves or things for other people

$pecial Projects

1. Identify three different economic choices that you or your family have had to make recently. Describe what your options were and why you made the choice you did.

2. Sometimes it is hard to make choices. Explain which purchasing decisions are hardest for you.

3. Make an attractive poster that illustrates choices a manufacturer might have to make or choices a consumer might face.

Money Decisions

While we might dream about having an unlimited supply of money, most people have more needs and wants than they have money to satisfy these desires. This means that they must constantly be making decisions about whether to spend money on one item instead of another. When they do this, they are deciding that one thing is more important to them than something else.

Look at the following choices and indicate what your decision would be if you were faced with these choices of how to spend money.

Would you decide:

_____ to go to the movie or _____ buy a book

_____ buy a new shirt or _____ buy a piece of sports equipment

_____ buy a gift for your mother or _____ go skating with your friends

_____ buy candy for yourself or _____ buy a card for a sick friend

_____ buy something to eat or _____ buy admission to a sports event

_____ buy a present for a friend's birthday or _____ buy the same thing for yourself

_____ get your hair cut or _____ buy a new piece of clothing

_____ take a friend out to lunch or _____ take a friend to a movie

_____ buy a plain pair of jeans or _____ buy a pair of designer jeans for twice the price

_____ buy two inexpensive toys that may break soon or buy one more expensive
      but durable toy

_____ buy a game that several people can play or _____ buy a computer game
      that you play by yourself

My Financial Personality

Indicate which statements best describe you and how you handle money. Then on the back of this paper write a short description of how you handle money.

I am a spendthrift.

I look for sales and good deals.

I spend every penny I get my hands on.

I am a penny pincher.

I only buy designer labels and brand names.

When I start a new hobby I want to have the best equipment.

I save some of my money.

Making money decisions makes me anxious.

I earn some of my spending money.

I expect my parents to pay for everything I want.

I like to save up until I can buy something worthwhile.

When I want something, I want it now and I don't care what it costs.

Wants and Needs

Because most people have a limited supply of money, they have to plan how they will spend their money. Some of the money goes for things they need — necessities. Some of the money goes for things they want but don't really need — luxuries. People usually spend their money on things they need before they buy luxury items.

What is a necessity?

_____

_____

List some of your family's necessities.

_____

_____

_____

_____

What is a luxury?

_____

_____

List some luxuries for your family.

_____

_____

_____

_____

Choose five luxuries. Assume that you have extra money to spend on luxuries. Rate these items from 1 to 5 (1 being your first choice and 5 your last choice) according to how you would spend the money. Ask two other people in your family to also rate how they would spend the money.

	my rating	other ratings	
_____	____	____	____
_____	____	____	____
_____	____	____	____
_____	____	____	____
_____	____	____	____

You're a Millionaire

Pretend that you have just inherited one million dollars. You immediately have to pay one third of that amount in taxes. How will you spend the remaining money? Make a list of purchases and prices (including sales tax if applicable).

item	price	remaining funds

When you are finished with your list, identify which purchases are needs and which are wants. Compare your list with a friend's list. What do the differences between your lists say about you and the things you think are important?

Your Budget

A budget is a way of planning how much money you expect to receive for a certain period (usually a month) and what expenses you expect to have during this time. It is usually just an estimate of your income and expenses. By making a budget you have a better idea of how much money you have to save for large expenses that don't happen every month and how much money you have left over for savings or luxuries.

Use this form to make a budget for yourself for one month. Add any categories that are not included that you feel are necessary. Then keep track of everything you spend during the month. At the end of the month tally all your expenses for each category and record them next to your budgeted figures for each category.

Budget for the month of _____

Estimated income _____

Expenses

	budgeted	actual
food	_____	_____
clothes	_____	_____
entertainment	_____	_____
music	_____	_____
lessons	_____	_____
equipment	_____	_____
hobbies	_____	_____
savings	_____	_____
charity	_____	_____
miscellaneous	_____	_____
total	_____	_____

A Family Budget

Use this worksheet to make a monthly budget for a family of four with a monthly income of $_____. You will have to use several sources of information (like newspapers) to get accurate estimates of the cost of housing, transportation, utilities and food in your community.

	budgeted amount
food	_____
housing	_____
transportation	_____
savings	_____
health care	_____
insurance	_____
utilities	_____
personal care	_____
clothes	_____
lessons/education	_____
entertainment	_____
miscellaneous	_____
total	_____

If this family receives 5% less income than they had expected for this month, which expenses could be reduced? Make a plan that would allow them to cover their necessary expenses with this reduced income.

Packaging Analysis

How many times do you buy products without really paying attention to why the product appeals to you? By reading labels on products and comparing ingredients and prices, you can make sure that you are getting the best buy for your money. For this activity you will look at a common product, cereal, and analyze the packaging and contents of several varieties of cereal.

For this activity you will need several other people. Everyone in your group should bring an empty cereal box. After you have your boxes, answer all these questions.

1. What cereal did you bring and why did you choose this cereal? _____

_____

2. What cereals did other people in your group bring? _____

_____

3. How many different manufacturers are represented in your group? _____

4. List the adjectives and phrases on your group's boxes

cereal name	descriptive words
_____	_____
_____	_____
_____	_____
_____	_____
_____	_____

5. What special offers (if any) are on your box of cereal? _____

_____

_____

6. Compare the costs your group's cereals.

cereal	cost	ounces	cost per ounce
_____	_____	_____	_____
_____	_____	_____	_____
_____	_____	_____	_____
_____	_____	_____	_____
_____	_____	_____	_____

Which cereal is the best value? _____

7. Compare the nutritional value of each cereal. Which cereal is the best? Why?

_____

_____

_____

8. Take a survey of your class members to find out which of your group's cereals is the favorite. On another piece of paper make a graph that shows the results of this survey.

$pecial Projects

1. Create your own cereal - As you create your new cereal, consider:
   - What are the main ingredients?
   - What will its name be?
   - What is the shape, color and/or texture?
   - What adjectives could you use to describe the cereal?

2. On a separate piece of paper, design a package for your cereal and create an advertisement to sell your new product.

You Pay for Convenience

You want a pizza. Do you take out all the ingredients and make one, pop a frozen pizza in the oven, or order a ready-to-eat pizza from a local restaurant? Many of the food products we buy are available in ready-to-eat form. This makes them quick and easy to use, but they often cost more than if you were to make yourself.

Select a product that is available in ready-made, frozen or packaged mix form and that can also be made "from scratch." Make a chart that compares the quality and the cost of preparing the item yourself versus buying the same item in a ready-to-make form.

Reading the Labels

If you are not in the habit of reading the labels on the items you purchase, you could be in for some disappointments. Most packaged foods provide information about nutrition and calories on the package or label. By checking the labels you can be sure that the brand you are buying is the best value and that it will meet your expectations.

Select one variety of food (cereal, juice, bread, jam, etc.) and compare the information on the labels from several brands. Write a summary of what you find about each product. Based on price per ounce and nutritional value, select the best product.

I studied the labels of _____

    Brand 1 _____

    _____

    _____

    Brand 2 _____

    _____

    _____

    Brand 3 _____

    _____

    _____

    The best product is_____

Supply and Demand

"**S**upply and demand" is a principle in economics that contends that in a competitive market the amount of a particular product that is available to consumers will determine the price. The **law of supply** says as the price of a good increases, producers will be willing to produce more of the good and as the price of a good decreases, producers will makes less. The **law of demand** says that, conversely, as the price increases, consumers will demand less, and as the price decreases, consumers will demand more. Together, these two laws relate the price of goods and the quantity available for purchase. If demand is greater than the available supply, businesses will be able to charge more and consumers will be paying more. When producers begin to produce more to meet the demand, this reduces the scarcity of the items and the price drops.

Draw arrows to complete this chart that shows the relationship between price, supply and demand.

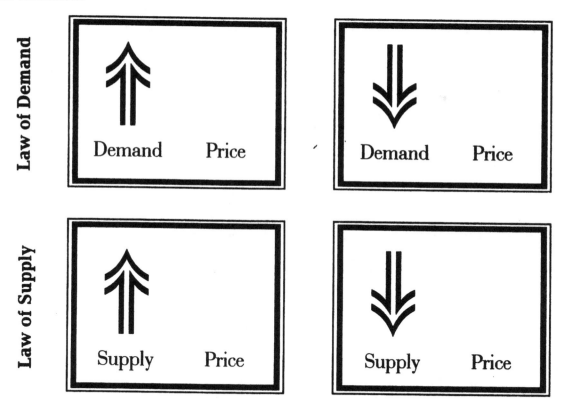

Give an example from real life to explain why these situations might happen.

decrease in supply _____

increase in supply_____

decrease in demand _____

increase in demand _____

To Market, To Market

Everything you buy, from food to complex computers, has gone through several stages of production before it ended up in your hands. At each stage of the production chain, someone does something to harvest, process, manufacture, or transport the raw material and make it available in its finished form for your purchase. Each of these people needs to be paid for his or her services.

Consider the banana in your lunch. Simple as it is, it went through several people's hands before it ended up in your possession. Before this piece of fruit came to be part of your lunch, it went through these stages:

■ plantation owner grows banana trees

■ workers harvest bananas

■ bananas are transported to your country

■ bananas are transported to your town

■ bananas are sold by the grocery store owner

$pecial Projects

Choose a common item (like a tennis shoe). On another piece of paper make a diagram that shows the steps that are involved with developing the product and making it available to the consumer.

© Prufrock Press Inc. — Money Matters

Buying on Credit

When people need to buy things and they don't have enough money, they often borrow the money. This is called buying on credit. When you buy on credit, you purchase goods and services and promise to pay for them in the future. People usually make big, expensive purchases, like cars and houses, on credit. When they use credit cards or get an advance on their pay checks they are also using credit.

Interest is the amount charged by the lender for the use of his or her money. The amount of interest paid is determined by the interest rate (% per year), the amount borrowed (principle) and the time of the loan (parts of a year). Simple interest is calculated by multiplying these three factors (**I = P x R x T**). The amount that must be repaid is the interest plus the amount borrowed.

On a loan of $200 at 7% for 2 years, you would have:

Interest = 200 x .07 x 2 = 28

The amount the borrower would have to repay would be $200 + $28, or a total of $228.

Figure the interest and the total amount of money that must be repaid.

1. Josh buys a surfboard for $600 at 12% interest. He repays the loan in 1 year.
   interest = _____   total amount paid = _____

2. Julia buys a diamond ring that costs $2,000. She borrows the money from her credit union at 10% interest for 2½ years.
   interest = _____   total amount paid = _____

3. Jordan overused his credit card and accumulated $3,000 in debt. The interest rate is 18% and he figures it will take him 2 years to pay it off.
   interest = _____   total amount paid = _____

4. Lucinda bought a new car for $15,000. The loan is at 10% for 5 years.
   interest = _____   total amount paid = _____

5. Grover bought a stereo for $600. He will repay the loan in 6 months at 15% interest.
   interest = _____   total amount paid = _____

Sample Check

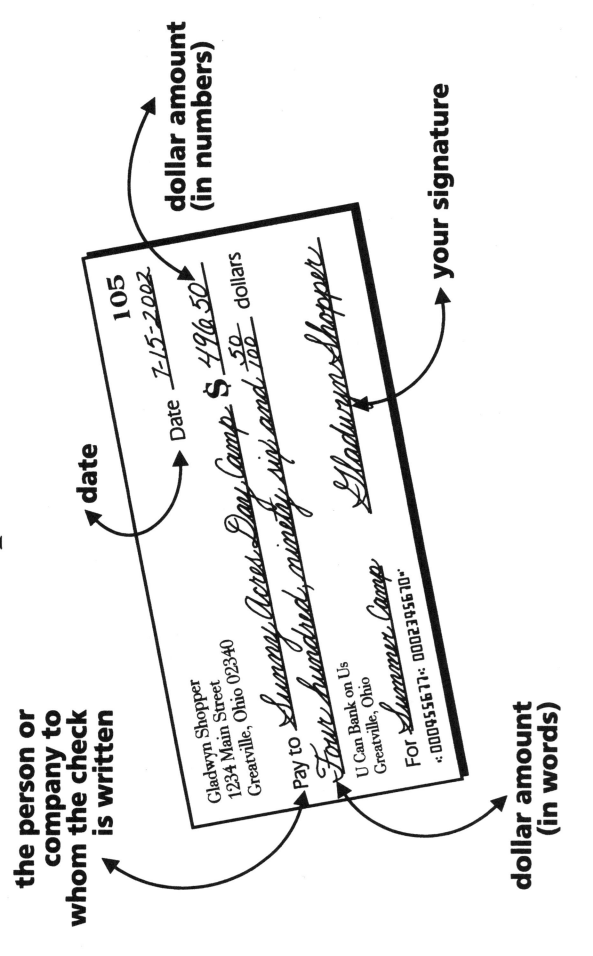

the person or company to whom the check is written

dollar amount (in numbers)

your signature

date

dollar amount (in words)

Gladwyn Shopper
1234 Main Street
Greatville, Ohio 02340

105

Date 2-15-2002

Pay to Sunny Acres Day Camp $ 496.50

Four hundred ninety six and 50/100 dollars

U Can Bank on Us
Greatville, Ohio

For Summer Camp

Gladwyn Shopper

⑆000955677⑆ 0002345670⑈

Let's Check It Out

Many people find it easier and safer to keep their money in a bank rather than carrying around cash. When they need to pay for items, they write a check. When the person to whom the check is written receives the check and presents it to his or her bank, he or she may get cash for the check or that amount can be credited to that person's account. It is important to not only write all the information on the check carefully and clearly, but also to keep track of all the checks you write so you will know how much money you have left in your bank account.

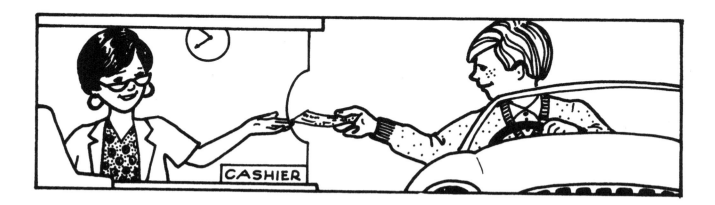

Make out a check for each of the following transactions and keep track of your expenditures in your account ledger. You have an opening balance in your checking account of $750.00. A deposit for $500.00 will have to be recorded, but do this only when you need it.

1. Varoom! . . . Only a few more months and that car will be all yours. The car payment of $323.00 can really drive you crazy. Ford of Oakdale likes to have its money on time. Please make out the payment by May 13th.

2. Spring is finally here, but winter left a mess in your yard. Leaves and broken trees are scattered around your property. The Green Thumb Yard Service will be out to clean up on May 15th and will only charge $236.75.

3. May 25th is your lucky day. An income tax refund of $410.39 arrives in the mail. Deposit it at once.

4. Payment for summer camp is due by June 1st. To reserve a place at the Sunny Acres Day Camp, make out a check for $496.50.

5. June 15th is coming and the mortgage payment of $329.62 is due. Pay to Rainbow Savings and Loan.

6. Mr. Harvey, your neighbor, doesn't look too happy since your baseball went through his front window. It's going to cost $52.52 to repair the window. White's Window Shop will do the job as soon as it receives the check.

Your Name   🚲   **101**

1234 Main Street
Anytown, Anyplace   Date _____

Pay to _____ $ _____

_____dollars

U Can Bank on Us
Your Town

For _____   _____

Your Name   🚲   **102**

1234 Main Street
Anytown, Anyplace   Date _____

Pay to _____ $ _____

_____dollars

U Can Bank on Us
Your Town

For _____   _____

Your Name   🚲   **103**

1234 Main Street
Anytown, Anyplace   Date _____

Pay to _____ $ _____

_____dollars

U Can Bank on Us
Your Town

For _____   _____

Your Name   🚲   **104**

1234 Main Street
Anytown, Anyplace   Date _____

Pay to _____ $ _____

_____dollars

U Can Bank on Us
Your Town

For _____   _____

Your Name
1234 Main Street
Anytown, Anyplace

105

Date _____

Pay to _____ $ _____

_____dollars

U Can Bank on Us
Your Town

For _____   _____

Your Name
1234 Main Street
Anytown, Anyplace

106

Date _____

Pay to _____ $ _____

_____dollars

U Can Bank on Us
Your Town

For _____   _____

Your Name
1234 Main Street
Anytown, Anyplace

Deposit Ticket

Date _____

Amount deposited $ _____

You Can Bank on Us
Your Town

Your Name
1234 Main Street
Anytown, Anyplace

Deposit Ticket

Date _____

Amount deposited $ _____

You Can Bank on Us
Your Town

Let's Check It Out
Record of Financial Transactions

number	date	transaction	payment (-)	deposit (+)	balance
		to _____			
		to _____			
		to _____			
		to _____			
		to _____			
		to _____			
		to _____			
		to _____			
		to _____			

Smart Buying

One important thing that smart consumers do is comparison shop. They look at different models or brands. They compare the prices at various stores. They talk to people who already own the product. They read information in product rating magazines and government agency publications. After doing all this research, they have enough information to make a good decision. If you are buying a small, inexpensive item, you can usually afford to make quick buying decisions; but if you are buying larger, more expensive items, it always pays to comparison shop.

Choose one of the five projects on these two pages. Your teacher will provide the amount of money you have to spend on each project.

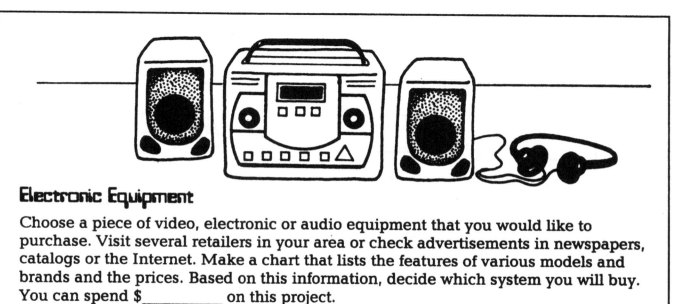

Electronic Equipment

Choose a piece of video, electronic or audio equipment that you would like to purchase. Visit several retailers in your area or check advertisements in newspapers, catalogs or the Internet. Make a chart that lists the features of various models and brands and the prices. Based on this information, decide which system you will buy. You can spend $_____ on this project.

Closet Clean Out

You need to clean out your closet, get rid of all your old, worn-out clothes, and get some new clothes. You will have to make a list of what articles of clothing you need to purchase. Then you're off to the store (or catalog or Internet) for a shopping spree that will put you in the height of fashion. Check several sources to find the best quality for the best price. Make a list of everything you will buy, where you will purchase it, and how much it will cost. Include pictures or drawings if you can. You have $_____ to spend on this project.

Car

Lucky you! You get to buy a new (or used) car. But before you head for the car lot or check out the newspaper ads, you will need to determine what your needs are (size, style, upkeep expense). Then you should consult a consumer magazine or car magazine for information that will help you make your decision. You will need to find several places where you can purchase a car and compare prices. When you present your project you should present your criteria for buying a car, the model you finally decided to buy, and where you will buy the car. If you choose to buy an older car that will need repairs or restoration, you should include estimates of these costs. You have $_____ to spend on this project.

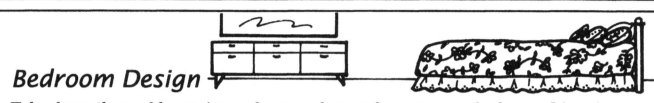

Bedroom Design

Take down those old curtains and get ready to redecorate your bedroom. It's going to be a whole new place when you get done. While you may not structurally alter the shape or size of the room, you may paint, wallpaper, change furniture and furnishings. Think carefully about what you want to do before you start and consult magazines and books for ideas. Your final presentation should include a floor plan of your remodeled room. This plan should show the changes you would like to make and include a cost analysis of all the materials and furnishings you will buy. Include pictures or samples if possible. You have $_____ to spend on this project.

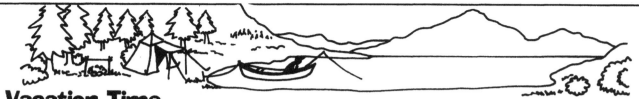

Vacation Time

School's out and it's time for a change of pace. You will be planning a week-long vacation for four people. You need to choose a place to visit, plan things to do while you are there, and figure all expenses for travel, lodging, meals, entrance fees, and any special equipment you may need to buy or rent. Some of the information on prices for airfares and lodging can be found on the Internet. In your final presentation, you should describe your destination, include an itinerary and map, and itemize all expenses. You can spend $_____ on this project.

Complaints

The manufacturers of products want consumers to be satisfied with their products. For this reason, many manufacturers will offer a guarantee that you will be satisfied. If you are not pleased with a product, you have the right to complain. There is, however, a correct way to complain. If you have a valid complaint, you should:

- Get organized. Collect all sales receipts (including the date of purchase), instruction booklets, and warranties. Know specifically why you are unhappy. Be prepared to describe in detail what the problem is.
- Return to the place where you purchased the item and ask to see the manager or consumer affairs department.
- State your problem clearly and calmly. Suggest a possible solution to the problem. Be sensible and don't make unreasonable demands. The store may exchange the item for another one, repair it, or refund your money either in cash or a store credit.

If you didn't buy the item locally or the local store won't respond, you must write to the manufacturer. The letter should include the following:

- your name, address and phone number
- date and place of purchase
- copies of the receipt, warranties, or previous letters (not the originals)
- an explanation of the problem
- description of the product (brand, model number, size)
- steps you've already taken to solve the problem
- suggested solution

$pecial Project

1. Write a letter of complaint to a manufacturer about a product (real or imaginary) that you are not satisfied with.

2. With a friend, act out a short skit that shows a person effectively presenting his or her problem with a defective product.

Ordering By Mail

Direct mail is any advertisement that is sent to your home through the mail. Shopping without leaving your home is convenient, and you can find unique items that are not available in your local stores. The drawbacks to this type of shopping are that it is sometimes hard to know what the product will be like (quality and size can be difficult to judge from a small picture in a catalog) and shipping charges can add a significant amount to the price of the item. Before you order anything through the mail, read the fine print. Be clear about what extra charges may be added to your order and what the company's return policy is.

Collect several direct-mail advertisements. Choose at least two products that are similar but sold by different companies. Analyze the products, the prices, the conditions of sale and the guarantees. Mount pictures of the products with your analysis. Explain which product you would advise someone to buy.

Company _____ **Product** _____

The facts _____

_____

_____

_____

_____

_____

_____

Company _____ **Product** _____

The facts _____

_____

_____

_____

_____

_____

42

Shopping on the Internet

Like direct mail shopping, Internet shopping can be convenient and can make a wide variety of products available to you. Shopping could be just a click away. But, as with all other forms of shopping, you need to be aware of what extra shipping or handling charges will be added to your merchandise and what the merchant's policies are if you are not satisfied with your purchase. Make sure the company includes an address and phone number you can use to get in touch with them should there be a problem. You will probably have to pay with a credit card, so make sure the site offers a secure transfer of information.

Choose an item that you would like to buy. Find two sites on the Internet where you can buy this item. Make a comparison of prices, extra charges, purchasing policies and return policies. On another piece of paper make a chart that compares the two companies.

product _____

	Company A	Company B
company name	_____	_____
Internet site	_____	_____
price	_____	_____
extra charges	_____	_____
	_____	_____
guarantee	_____	_____
	_____	_____
	_____	_____
other factors	_____	_____
	_____	_____
	_____	_____

Rent or Buy?

When you rent something, you pay for its temporary use. There are many things that you do not have to buy; you can rent them. The things you can rent range from housing and cars to clothing. There are many times when it makes sense to rent an item rather than buy it. This is especially true when you need an item for only a short period of time or when you do not have enough money to buy the item.

Research the advantages and disadvantages of renting versus buying. Choose two of the following items and check on cost, time limits and special restrictions on renting the item.

- car
- furniture
- yard equipment
- tuxedo
- sporting equipment
- television
- video recordings
- housing

Renting a _____

Information

_____

_____

_____

_____

_____

_____

Is it better to rent or buy?

_____

_____

Renting a _____

Information

_____

_____

_____

_____

_____

_____

Is it better to rent or buy?

_____

_____

What guidelines would you suggest for people who are trying to decide whether to rent or buy merchandise? _____

_____

_____

Economic Systems

Economy refers to how a nation uses its resources (goods and services). It involves decisions about what, how, and for whom products should be produced. Economies are generally divided into those that advocate private ownership and those that give the central government control over the production and distribution of goods. The three main types of economies are:

capitalism - In this system, individuals own the businesses and make decisions about what will be produced. In a completely capitalistic system, there would be no government regulation or intervention in the country's economy. This is sometimes called a free market system.

socialism - In this system, the government owns some of the larger industries and may also establish wages and policies for workers. The government may also collect taxes to provide social benefits for all people (health care, retirement, welfare).

communism - With communism the government owns all businesses and controls the distribution of goods produced. In some communistic economies all property, including housing, may be held by the government. In a strict communistic economy, all private ownership would be abolished and production, prices, and wages would be set by the government.

$Special Projects

1. Do additional research on these three different types of economies. Decide what you think should be government's role in the distribution of wealth, monitoring and regulating price and production, and establishing safety and purity standards. Write a letter to your congressional representative and explain your views.

2. Make a chart that shows the differences between these systems and describes how each system works. Write an analysis that tells which system does the following:
   - offers the fairest distribution of goods and services
   - offers the largest selection of goods and services.

Pinching Pennies

There are basically two ways you can have more money at the end of the month. You can make more money (increase income) or you can spend less (decrease expenditures). Often it is much easier to control what you spend than to increase your income. If you think about it, there are many easy ways that you (or your family) could reduce the amount of money you spend.

Find a variety of sources of information for ways to save money. Brainstorm ideas that you think are interesting and feasible. Choose the best ones to make a list of ideas that people your age could implement.

Penny Pinchers' Platform

Money Smarts

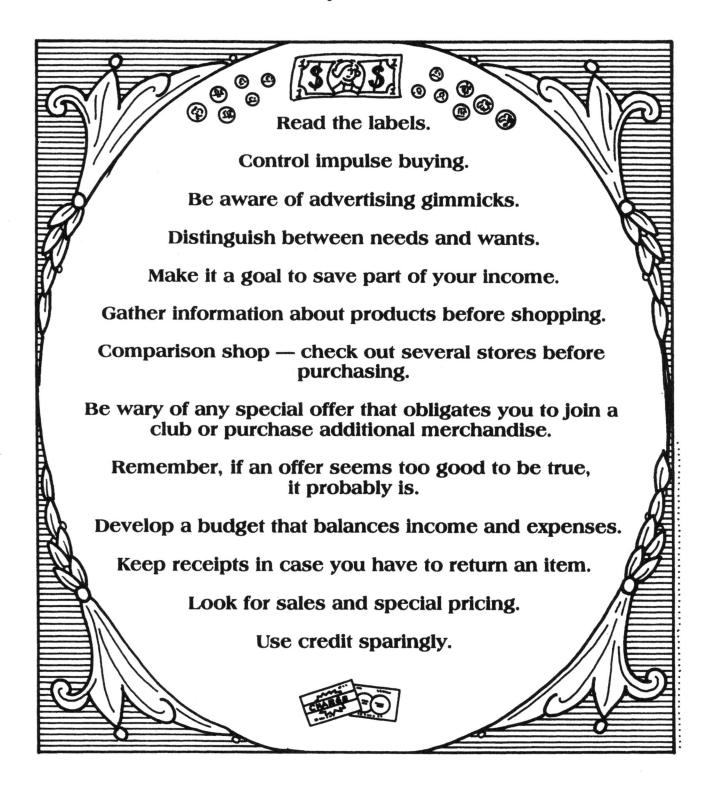

Read the labels.

Control impulse buying.

Be aware of advertising gimmicks.

Distinguish between needs and wants.

Make it a goal to save part of your income.

Gather information about products before shopping.

Comparison shop — check out several stores before purchasing.

Be wary of any special offer that obligates you to join a club or purchase additional merchandise.

Remember, if an offer seems too good to be true, it probably is.

Develop a budget that balances income and expenses.

Keep receipts in case you have to return an item.

Look for sales and special pricing.

Use credit sparingly.

CPSIA information can be obtained
at www.ICGtesting.com
Printed in the USA
LVHW100507121218
600076LV00015BA/542/P